THE Argus BOOK OF
CAPE TOWN

THE Argus BOOK OF
CAPE TOWN

STRUIK
PUBLISHERS

Struik Publishers

An operating division of
The Struik Group (Pty) Ltd
Struik House, Oswald Pirow Street
Foreshore, Cape Town 8001

Registration No 80/02842/07

First published 1988

House editor: Jan Schaafsma
Design: Janice Evans
Cover design: Abdul Amien

Typesetting by Diatype Setting cc, Cape Town
Reproduction by Sparhams Cape, Cape Town
Printed and bound by CTP Book Printers (Pty) Ltd, Parow

ISBN 0 86977 392 5

Front cover: Illuminated Table Mountain looms behind what was once busy, bustling District Six. Now only forlorn churches and mosques remain.
Back Cover: Table Mountain forms an impressive backdrop to most parts of the Cape Peninsula; The city wears a bright face at carnival time; A historical monument in Stellenbosch's Dorp Street; Yacht racing has become a popular sport in Table Bay and Cape sailors have competed successfully in major races in every ocean.
Half title page: Tall office blocks give South Africa's oldest city a modern look.
Title page: The city's lights are reflected in the calm water of Three Anchor Bay.
This page: The lion stares out to sea, with Sea Point nestling against its right flank and the Twelve Apostles to the left.

FOREWORD

PHOTOGRAPHERS OF *The Argus* NEWSPAPER see more of life than most. That goes with the job, of course, for it is their assignment to be here, there and everywhere – for the record. This book is part, albeit a generally more attractive and gentler part, of that photographic record.

A vital component of creating the overall picture of the life and times of Cape Town and its surrounds is the alertness, the 'eye for the moment' and the skill of those cameramen who watch over it and document, on film, the great events and the ordinary ones.

Truly memorable newspaper pictures are those which are seized in an instant; at a precise moment, never to be repeated, but captured forever. That may happen through professional instinct, anticipation and instant reflexes. Or it may even be sheer chance and, yes, luck.

Whatever the circumstances, newspaper pictures are about the unusual and the dramatic; about the contrasts in the patchwork of society, the joy and the grief, humour and hurt, squalor and splendour, the beauty and the beast.

They are a special breed, these photographers. Perhaps versatility is what it takes; a mix of talent and tenacity, creativity and courage. It is a matter of record that *The Argus* photographic team is widely recognised for its achievements and excellence. Among those who serve our readers now, as with others in the past, are award-winners both nationally and internationally.

Here, now, is a segment of their portfolio, one which captures the essence of Cape Town. There is little formality or studied elegance about this full-colour gallery of a vibrant place – the cosmopolitan Cape; complex, mostly beautiful, sometimes tragically sad, often cheerful, but always compelling.

Argus photographers whose work is featured are Jim McLagan, Dana le Roux, Willie de Klerk, Peter Stanford, Doug Pithey, Hannes Thiart, Dion Tromp and Leon Müller. The text and captions are by David Biggs, daily columnist of *The Argus*.

ANDREW DRYSDALE
Editor, The Argus

1

INTRODUCTION

2

SIR FRANCIS DRAKE CALLED IT 'the Fairest Cape in the whole circumference of the earth'. Bartholomeu Dias called it 'Cabo Tormentoso' – the Cape of Storms. Later it became known as the Cape of Good Hope. The Cape Peninsula is all these – a breathtakingly beautiful finger of land pointing into the raging wilderness of the southern oceans. Unpredictably moody, unbelievably serene, the Cape is as wanton as a child – and every bit as charming.

Table Mountain, the sandstone matriarch which spreads its protective arms around the city huddled on its slopes, is far more than just a famous tourist attraction or the subject of a thousand pretty postcards. It embodies the unique and irresistable character of the Cape, with all its rapid swings of mood. When a fire breaks out on the mountain's slopes, the people of Cape Town wear long faces. This is *their* mountain, and its moods are their moods.

Old Cape sea-dogs like to brag: 'We don't have a climate in the Cape. We just have *weather*.' And the real force behind the weather is the wind which batters the peninsula from all sides. In winter the moisture-laden northwester hurls itself against the northern slopes of Table Mountain; in summer the southeaster furiously hammers

the steep southern slopes, sweeping up the damp sea air to cover the heights with a downward-swirling mantle of thick cloud.

On the Newlands side the mountain helps to produce some of the highest rainfall figures in South Africa. On the city side the mountain helps create the dramatic white 'table cloth' which often decorates the mountain top on summer days.

Like the mountain, the city is a place of sharp contrasts and changing moods. Gracious old Victorian buildings rub shoulders with stark modern granite and glass office blocks. On the Foreshore at the lower end of Adderley Street these sombre, ashen-faced towers stand solemnly in line, as if self-consciously aware of their own importance. At the other end of the street the buildings are more spirited, their ornately-decorated windows, columns, niches and statuary testifying to a more exuberant age.

And in the Company Gardens, a short stroll from the commercial centre of the city, old men dream on shady benches or play quiet games of chess; lovers kiss, oblivious of the passing parade; and children feed the friendly squirrels.

One of the really delightful features of Cape Town is that any part of the busy city is only a few minutes drive away from complete rural tranquillity. Weekends and holidays find Capetonians flocking out to the unspoiled areas like Kirstenbosch Gardens, Newlands forest, or the long, sun-splashed beaches at Milnerton, Muizenberg, Kommetjie or Scarborough. And for many Table Mountain provides endless pleasure, whether for strenuous climbing or leisurely strolling.

There's always space to be alone if you want to.

1. Light fantastic. The dying glow of a summer evening adds its soft light to the sparkle of the city. Three glowing lines of street lights mark the main arteries that carry its lifeblood – the thousands of workers – into the heart of Cape Town each day.
2. Every year the Table Mountain cableway takes thousands of tourists to the top for a bird's eye view of the city.

2

TAVERN OF THE SEAS

THE FIRST EUROPEAN VISITORS TO THE Cape of Good Hope came to establish a tavern – a resting place where travellers could break their long journey to the East. Voyages in those days of simple square-rigged ships were long, tedious affairs that lasted many months at sea without fresh food or water. This often resulted in illness, and sometimes in death.

If the spice route to the East was to become a reality, there would have to be a stopping place where ships could be repaired, fresh food and water taken aboard, and ailing sailors nursed back to health. Table Bay provided such a tavern. It could supply all the needs of the passing ships. There were tall, indigenous trees nearby for timber, a stream of fresh water which ran from the lower slopes of the mountain into the bay, and plenty of animals to provide meat. Once the first settlers had established a garden, they could supply fruit and vegetables to the ships that called.

Today Table Bay Harbour is still a welcome port of call for many ships, even though the great days of the regular passenger liners and mail ships have passed. But some of Cape Town's older residents shake their heads sadly and say things will never be the same. Since the demise of the regular mail ship run the harbour has lost its busy, bustling character. Over the years ships and ship handling have changed. Before containerisation arrived it took a week to unload and load a big cargo ship. Cranes swung their great nets of bales and crates out of the holds, and teams of stevedores wrestled them on to waiting railway trucks. The docks echoed with shouted instructions and profanities, and great numbers of sailors enjoyed their weeks ashore.

Today's ships can load and unload in a matter of hours. Diesel motors are relatively clean and ships require very small crews. Modern mariners work in conditions closer to those in a city office than those in the dirty, clanging steamships. There are no rough crews of coal-dust stained sailors eager for a few nights of shore-life after long weeks of hardship at sea.

But the tavern spirit lives on. Visiting yachtsmen from all corners of the world agree that a call at the Cape is a highlight of any voyage. Fleets of foreign fishing trawlers find the harbour a place of friendships (and sometimes, of course, of fights as well, as in any waterfront community). Many ships call in for repairs in the harbour's large dry dock. The cranes might be idle, but the work of serving ships goes on. One of the obvious changes to this service has been the introduction of helicopters. Many of the great tankers served by Table Bay Harbour do not even stop here. Helicopters fly out to them as they pass, dropping mail, spares or medical supplies, thus avoiding the need for an expensive and time-consuming stopover.

1. On a calm evening, not even a breeze ripples the water as it reflects the city lights.
2. A busy workboat scurries by as a graceful Scandinavian liner comes in to dock.
3. The popular 'Penny Ferry' retains a touch of traditional charm in a changing harbour.

One of the most often-heard complaints about Cape Town is that the harbour is not linked with the city, so the people of Cape Town have no feeling of belonging to the sea. The great pier that once reached out from the foot of Adderley Street into the harbour has gone. A wide system of multi-lane highways and flyover bridges now forms a physical and psychological barrier between the people and the port. The most recent plans for the harbour are aimed at bringing the city people back to the sea, and this is as it should be, for the harbour is the reason for the city's existence.

In recent years yachting has become a major South African sport. Sailors such as Bruce Dalling, Bertie Reid and John Martin have helped to put the country firmly on the international yachting map. South African skippers feature among the leaders of many of the world's great ocean races. This has stimulated widespread interest in yachting, and every Cape suburb has its fleet of fibreglass dreams growing in backyards as would-be skippers put the finishing touches to their home-built boats. Cape Town's yacht fleet grows larger every year. Mooring at the Peninsula's yacht clubs have become crowded and expensive, and there are plans to increase the space available to small boat owners in the harbour. When these become a reality, Table Bay Harbour will be a very different place; a place for the people of Cape Town and not merely for those who are passing through.

Seasoned travellers all over the world know you can judge a good tavern by the fact that it serves the local residents as well as those who come only for one night's shelter. Table Bay was once such a tavern. It looks set to become one again.

2

1. The Cape's yacht fleet is growing rapidly as the sport gains in popularity, and moorings have become very crowded.
2. Local yachtsmen, trained in the stormy southern Atlantic waters, have fared well in major ocean races. Springbok skipper John Martin stands at the helm.
3. Table Bay is a hospitable port of call for international sailors. Here small boats escort a graceful old sailing vessel as she sets sail for Australia.
4. Billowing spinnakers and sparkling water. Sailing days like this make it easy to see why competition yachting has become so popular at the Cape.

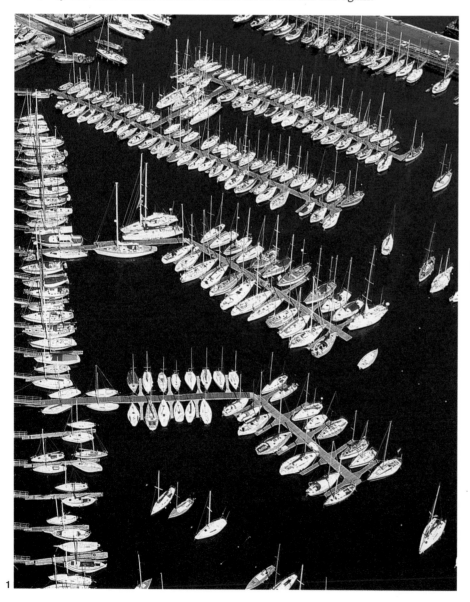

1

3 4

2

3

1. The mailships no longer call and most of the harbour cranes stand idle, but there's still plenty of activity in the oldest part of Cape Town's Table Bay Harbour. Here small working craft ply their daily trade, fishing, ferrying and servicing larger vessels anchored in the bay.

2. The worldwide search for oil has made giant rigs like this a common sight in Table Bay, where they are often berthed for repairs or refits. This rig's own powerful crane winches up a crate of spares from a harbour ferry, while the sturdy legs form a frame for Table Mountain.

3. Modern warehouses and fuel tanks dwarf the picturesque little clock tower at the entrance to Cape Town's Victoria Basin. Once the harbourmaster office, it now houses the museum of the Ship Society.

CITY BOWL

THE CURVED, CRAGGY FACE OF TABLE MOUNTAIN, with Devil's Peak at one end and Lion's Head and Signal Hill at the other, forms the rim of the bowl in which the heart of Cape Town lies. This is the oldest part of the city, where the first streets were laid out, and the first open spaces planned, so farmers could turn their unwieldy teams of oxen when they came to town with their produce. In Greenmarket Square they could outspan their teams and set up camp while the townsfolk came to make their purchases.

In the early days it was a differently shaped bowl. The sea lapped at the feet of the Castle walls and all of what is today known as the Foreshore was under water. This large expanse of shallow water made it impossible for ships to come close inshore to discharge their passengers and cargo, so the land was eventually reclaimed, moving the sea's edge back until a suitable harbour could be built, deep enough to accommodate an ocean-going ship.

The ox-wagons and the sailing ships are long gone now, and the Castle stands some distance from the sea, but much remains to remind us of those early days. The garden laid out by the Dutch East India Company is still there, although it now provides relaxation, rather than vegetables. Greenmarket Square is a market once again, although the traders are no longer farmers with eggs and butter for sale, but vendors in market stalls offering a fascinating variety of handmade goods, leatherwork, jewellery, bright clothing, old books, buttons, badges and trinkets.

Street markets and street entertainments have become a permanent and fascinating feature of life in central Cape Town. Lively groups of drummers and dancers from the black townships bring a carnival atmosphere to the city centre, with well-attended lunch-time performances in Greenmarket Square, while saxophone players, flautists, singers and tap-dancers woo the passing parade with their talents. Most of the musicians earn a reasonable living from passersby, and their instrument cases are soon lined with coins. The biggest street markets are in Greenmarket Square, Church Street and at the Railway Station. Fruit and vegetable sellers have pitches on almost every street and there is a large and regular produce market on the Parade.

This swing towards small business enterprises has been one of the most marked changes in the city centre in recent years. Even the 'public transport' has gone private with the introduction of hundreds of individually-owned minibus taxis serving commuters from the black townships. A large section of Strand Street has been set aside for the use of these informal bus operators.

1. Cape Town – mixing bowl of cultures and centuries.
2. Jan van Riebeeck stands unchanging as the city changes round him.
3. The old City Hall recalls a richer, more gracious age.
4. Clowns and carnivals. The Mother City can still put on a youthful face.

2

Many of Cape Town's oldest and most gracious buildings have been preserved and restored, while some areas have been developed in modern style, sometimes with unfortunate results. Cape Town's Foreshore is a conglomerate of gloomy modern buildings in various shades of grey and it isn't surprising that the people of the city feel cut off from the sea. Such a solid barricade of greyness must present something of a psychological barrier.

Closer to the mountain, however, you get a better idea of what Cape Town must have looked like in gentler times. Here are fine old buildings, obviously built for posterity, with flowing lines wrought in granite, iron and teak. Many of them are adorned with interesting statuary, turrets and balconies which may present a headache for cleaners, but are certainly a delight for the city's pigeons.

Of course, not all of Cape Town's modern buildings are an eyesore. In recent times some very attractive new buildings have been designed to blend happily with their older neighbours, proving that young and old can exist in harmony.

Probably the most interesting street in the city centre is Long Street, which is packed from end to end with an assortment of unusual speciality shops, from computer suppliers to bead specialists. Here you will find wool shops, pawn shops, second hand clothing stores and even a shop selling the country's finest boerewors. Most of these old shops have been restored to lacy Victorian splendour, and the street is a hive of cheerful commercial activity.

As in the rest of the Cape Peninsula, the weather plays an important role in the city centre's life. On rainy days the street market stalls are packed away and the street musicians stay at home. And when the southeaster whips furiously through the city, frail old women are grateful for the steadying hand of a traffic officer; sometimes traffic officers themselves are happy to find a heavy pedestrian to cling to if there isn't a pole nearby. The strength of the southeaster, known locally as the 'Cape Doctor', must be experienced to be believed.

But whatever the weather, at noon each day the cannon on Signal Hill booms out over the city, flocks of startled pigeons take to the air, and old Capetonians say this is when you can recognise a visitor to the city without any trouble at all. They're the ones who do not automatically glance at their watches.

3

1. Cape Town's flower sellers add a cheerful splash of colour.
2. For fabric bargains, the Grand Parade is hard to beat.
3. At the end of a busy day, *The Argus* goes home to the suburbs.
4. An alfresco exhibition in Government Avenue.

1. There's music for every ear – throbbing skins in the square . . .
2. . . . the precision of the corps de ballet in the Nico Malan . . .
3. . . . a symphony concert in the City Hall . . .
4. . . . or the colourful chorus of the Coon Carnival at New Year.

4

1

2

3

1. Cape Town's weather changes fast. It can be awesome, stunningly beautiful or just wet and cold. Here swirling evening clouds capture the sunset to create fantastic sculptures in the sky above Kloof Nek, between Table Mountain and Lion's Head.
2. On a wet winter evening the statues in the gardens have the place to themselves as the paths fill with pools of light and puddles of fresh rainwater.
3. When the Cape south-easter blows, wise pedestrians grab something solid to hang on to. This traffic officer finds a secure anchor in the form of a portly pedestrian.
4. Storm clouds lift and a bright rainbow raises its colours over the rain-washed city.

1. A city at night has a fascination all its own, and Cape Town is no exception. On the Foreshore, the fountain combines water with light to create an evening spectacle.
2. Adderley Street's festive lights provide a special treat for summer visitors every year.
3. A highlight of the city's annual festival is the fireworks display over the harbour.

4

1. Cape Town's best known religious leader is Archbishop Desmond Tutu.
2. Young worshippers on their way to one of many attractive mosques.
3. The Cape's Islamic community is a large and vigorous one.

4. Under the tall, illuminated Christmas tree in Greenmarket Square, children sing carols by candlelight.

1. Cape Town has recently experienced a renaissance of exciting architectural designs, as this fine modern block shows. A series of roof gardens at varying levels enables the tenants to make full use of the Cape's fine weather.

2. Old and new styles rub shoulders in the city centre. Stark modern granite and glass contrast with the ornate plaster and mouldings of a Victorian office block.

3. The Castle, Cape Town's oldest building, is rich in history and tradition, but remains in daily use as a military headquarters and popular tourist attraction.

4. Careful restoration has brought many of the city's old Victorian buildings back to their former splendour. These richly ornamented gables are set against the mathematical precision of a modern concrete office block.

5. A double highway carries traffic under the new Civic Centre, which houses the city's municipal offices. A pedestrian way also crosses the highway to link the Nico Malan Opera House to the rest of the city.

3

4

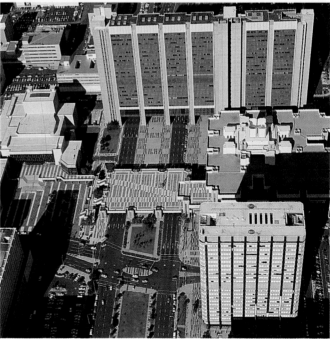

5

1

2

3

4

1. Cape Town, South Africa's legislative capital, has seen many changes of government – and of style of government. Here the three houses of Parliament meet for the first time in the chamber designed for this new style of law-making.
2. White helmets gleam and boots ring out on the freshly cobbled square as the guards are changed outside the Houses of Parliament.
3. Seated stiffly outside the Parliament buildings, where he once served with distinction as the country's Prime Minister, Jan Smuts stares down Adderley Street over the heads of the pedestrians.
4. The State President's Guard adds a touch of military pageantry to Stalplein, outside Parliament.
5. Bright beds of flowers provide an appropriate touch to Tuynhuys, official office of the State President.

5

1

2

3

For the very young and the very old, there's time to stop and stare; time to chat and share, but for those in between, life must go on at the frantic pace of the modern city.

1. A pause for reflection as children come face to face with themselves in a plate glass window. For little girls, it's a chance for a critical close-up examination. Any wrinkles yet? Little boys don't let anything interrupt a long, cool drink.
2. After a hectic day of dealing with clients, or typing the boss' dictated letters, the final hurdle is the rush for the train home.
3. On a summer morning there's time for Granny to sit on the Parade and chat to a friend before buying the week's vegetables at one of the many food stalls.
4. Two wheels help to beat the traffic and a pair of brightly coloured cycling pants provides high visibility – very necessary when there are cars roaring past.

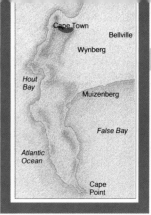

TABLE MOUNTAIN

TABLE MOUNTAIN HAS BECOME A SYMBOL of the Cape. This immense, brooding block of rock looms over the Mother City, governing her moods – and her weather.

The people of Cape Town have always regarded Table Mountain as their own. Tourists may take the cableway to the summit and stare in wonder at the vista of sea and city spread out at their feet, but Capetonians love the mountain, and live on it. On weekends hundreds of hikers of all ages tread the winding paths along the mountain slopes. These provide a wide variety of routes for strollers and experienced climbers alike.

Some adventurers prefer the heady delights of scaling the sheer rock faces. And every year there are one or two who underestimate the might of Table Mountain and are brought home on stretchers. Over the years the Mountain Club and the Cape's efficient Metro Rescue organisation have become experienced at locating and retrieving casualties – dead or alive. Some intrepid flyers use the mountain as a launching ramp, leaping from it to soar down to Mouille Point on fragile hang-gliders.

The Table Mountain Cableway is one of South Africa's best known tourist attractions, and on clear summer days long queues of visitors patiently wait their turn to take the swaying cable car on its spider web ascent to the summit. For some newcomers this is a terrifying ride, but for others it's all part of a day's work. Every morning a cableway technician rides the route to the top and back, perched nonchalantly on top of the car as he inspects the thick cable for signs of wear.

When the southeaster spreads the white table cloth of cloud over the top of the mountain – an event which can happen startlingly fast, the siren sounds to announce the closing of the cableway, and visitors at the top are brought down through the chilly mist. Legend has it that this table cloth of cloud is actually the smoke from a furious smoking contest between the devil and the Cape's best-known tobacco addict, Mr Van Hunks. They have been puffing away for centuries. But smoke of a more serious nature is sometimes seen on the mountain slopes – the smoke of a bush fire. The Cape is windy for most of the year, and the mountain is naturally a windier place than most, so any mountain fire is likely to spread fast. Wind-blown sparks leap ahead of the fire line to start fresh blazes hundreds of metres away, making the task of firefighting teams very difficult and dangerous. When the mountain burns, the people of Cape Town suffer as though they were also being licked by flames. Few things sadden true Capetonians as much as the sight of blackened patches of burned mountain vegetation after a fire.

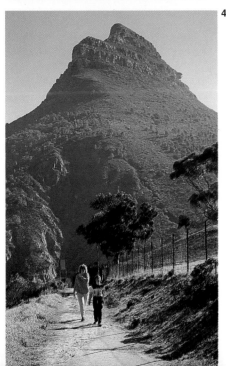

1. The top of Table Mountain, from where visitors get a bird's eye view of the city below.
2. From this vantage point the city and Table Bay are spread out like a vast map.
3. All in a day's work. A technician takes a high ride to check the smooth running of the cableway.
4. The slopes of the mountain are criss-crossed with attractive paths for hikers.

The variety of vegetation on Table Mountain is one of the richest in the world, and even to non-botanists the number of wild flowers is breathtaking. Apart from the spectacular proteas, there are no fewer than 102 species of erica found on the Peninsula. Not even the fierce mountain fires have detracted from this floral treasure, and some species actually seem to thrive on regular burning. Others, like the graceful silver tree, which is indigenous to the slopes of Table Mountain, have been seriously threatened by fires and competition from alien vegetation. Botanists, however, have succeeded in propagating silver trees in other areas, so they are not threatened with total extinction.

Cape Town's Table Mountain is many things to many people. Some may take the cableway to the top and back, but there are others who prefer a more exciting trip.

1. This intrepid climber sways from his rope above empty space, like a spider in its web.
2. Others leap from the mountain to soar like brightly coloured birds.
3. Not all decents are smooth, as members of the Mountain Club can tell you. Each year the mountain claims its victims.
4. Table Mountain attracts the adventurous. Here a rock climber feels for a finger-hold on a vertical face high above the clouds.

4

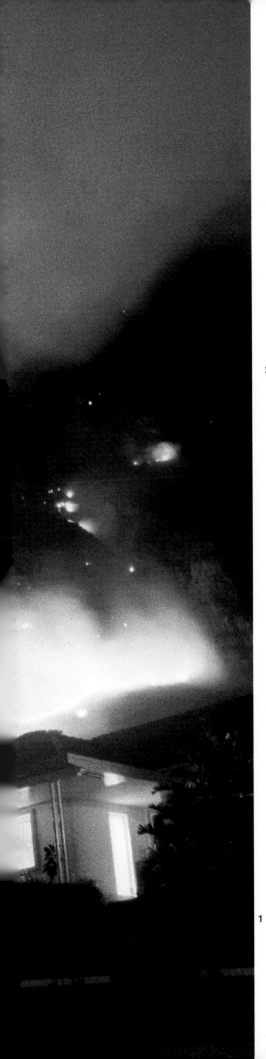

1. Mountain fires are anxious times for Cape Town residents, particularly those with homes on the mountain slopes.
2. Smouldering logs can easily flare up to start new fires, so each one must be extinguished.
3. Fires leave ugly scars that can take many months to heal.
4. The Cape's floral kingdom is one of the richest in the world. It is fortunate that it usually recovers well after a fire.

Overleaf: On a warm summer evening an illuminated mountain face provides a dramatic backdrop to a glittering bowl of city lights.

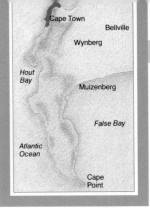

ATLANTIC COAST

ON THE WESTERN SLOPES OF THE MOUNTAIN LIE THE bustling, cosmopolitan suburbs of Sea Point, Green Point and Camps Bay. Sea Point is a suburb of soaring blocks of modern flats, fashionable boutiques, synagogues, delicatessens and restaurants to suit every palate and pocket. Here visitors can choose a meal from a range that includes Italian, Greek, Swiss, Bavarian, French and American fare. Restaurants rise and fall in popularity, and when one closes down, it is invariably replaced by another. At the pavement cafes you can hear a variety of languages being spoken and World Cup soccer matches are matters of personal involvement.

Cape Town's city centre dies at 5 pm, but Sea Point comes alive. This is the side of the Peninsula where the sun sets, and sunset is socialising time in Sea Point. The residents of high-rise flats promenade on the sea front with their pampered dogs. Friends meet and greet loudly. Joggers, combining fitness with fashion, select their designer track-suits to show off their figures to the best advantage. Blue-haired matrons discuss their grandchildren, and businessmen wearing floral shirts, shorts and sandals conclude deals over a beachfront cup of coffee. And the gulls are never far away, ready to snatch a snack from the plate of any unwary alfresco diner. The voices are loud, the music is louder. You're as likely to hear Yiddish, German or Greek as you are to hear English or Afrikaans.

Because most of the residents of the Sea Point side live in flats, the sea front promenade, with its wide stretch of well clipped lawn and its paved walkway and park benches, is regarded as everybody's front garden. Mothers and nannies watch as small children play on the grass, young men organise games of touch rugby or cricket and many stroll and chat or just stand and watch.

At Graaff's Pool an informal club of middle-aged regulars meet each morning or evening for a nude swim in the icy water, sheltered from prying eyes by a weathered concrete wall. Further along the coast, Clifton's Fourth Beach is the traditional spot for younger sunworshippers. Summer's smell is suntan oil and ice-cream and summer's dress is sunglasses and bikini – as brief as the figure allows, and sometimes briefer. Young men look up critically from their magazines and survey the 'talent' through mirrored lenses. Strangely enough, while a female figure that's less than perfect sometimes raises disapproving eyebrows, males seem quite happy to display vast expanses of beer-filled belly. There is no equality of the sexes on a beach.

1

4

1. Sea Point's beachfront flat-land gives residents ready access to beaches and tidal pools.
2. The lighthouse at Mouille Point is always on duty, protecting ships in darkness and fog.
3. Flatland residents meet on the promenade to admire babies, dogs and other residents . . .
4. . . . or to watch a spectacular sunset, while a powerskier gets an even closer view.

Closer to the city, Green Point is home to several sports clubs. Here, on a wide expanse of open parkland, a soccer stadium, golf course, tennis courts and bowling greens have been established. Nearby is the site of one of the country's best-known lighthouses, the Mouille Point Lighthouse. When the cold fog descends over Table Bay, the mournful moan of the Mouille Point fog-horn is a familiar noise, reminding residents that the sea is not only a place for bikinis and surfboards, but also a place where men risk their lives, making a living on trawlers and tankers. And the rocky coastline claims its share of ships every year.

1. On summer days bright umbrellas blossom on the beaches and the air is filled with the aroma of hot sun-tan oil. At weekends there's hardly room to swing a tanga . . .

2. . . . unless it's a very small tanga, in which case we can always find a bit more space. A warm rock offers an ideal spot to dry off and soak up the sunshine after a dip in the chilly Atlantic Ocean.

3. Whenever you find pretty girls on a beach, you'll find boys going to extraordinary lengths to attract their attention. Some even defy gravity . . .

4. . . . but who needs boys on the beach, anyway, when you have a good friend to hold your hand and take you for a walk?

Overleaf: The summer evening shadows lengthen on Clifton Beach and the holiday visitors go home to their hotels for dinner, leaving the sand, trampled but deserted, for the residents to enjoy.

1. Evenings and nights have their own magic on the Peninsula's Atlantic coast. Lights splash down on seawashed rocks, painting them an eery green. Across Bantry Bay brightly lit buildings are reflected in the smooth dark water. And above it all, the dark mountain broods.

2. Dogs and their owners enjoy a cooling paddle in the sea as the evening shadows lengthen on the sand. One side of Sea Point life comes to a gentle close . . .

3. . . . while the other side bursts into brightly-lit action. Sea Point's restaurants and cafes provide for every taste and pocket. Some provide music, drinking and dancing, while others cater for those who simply want to sip and watch the crowds go by.

The mountains and the sea give Cape Town its unique character and those who cannot live by the sea or on the slopes of the mountains make full use of them when it's time for relaxing.

1. Some are lucky enough – or rich enough – to have their castles in the air, like this spectacular home perched high among the boulders above the Atlantic at Llandudno.
2. The sea belongs to everybody, and for those with a taste for adventure, there's usually enough wind and waves to provide plenty of fast action.
3. The traditional postcard view of Table Mountain is this one from the Bloubergstrand side of Table Bay. The photographer has framed the cloudtopped mountain in a blaze of bright aloes.

2 3

HOUT BAY AND CONSTANTIA

THE FERTILE CONSTANTIA VALLEY IS THE BIRTHPLACE of South Africa's wine industry. Here Simon van der Stel laid out the vineyards and established the elegant homestead which he called Constantia.

Mystery surrounds the name Constantia. Van der Stel's records make no mention of the woman whose name inspired him. She certainly wasn't his wife: he had left her behind in Holland, and anyway, her name wasn't Constantia. The more prosaically minded believe that it honoured the daughter of the obscure official who made the original land grant, and that its allegorical meaning ('constancy') also played a part. However, one Stellenbosch historian suggests that Constantia commemorates a great love affair, and this is appropriate. Good wine and lovely women have always been associated.

Some years ago plans were passed to turn most of the Constantia valley into a high-density residential area. But a trust company was formed and land was bought and turned into what is now Buitenverwachting wine farm. The march of the town houses was halted. Today almost all of Van der Stel's original Constantia is again producing wine grapes. It now consists of three farms, Groot Constantia, Klein Constantia and Buitenverwachting.

A tribute to Van der Stel's farming skill is that the modern owners of the farms say that if they had to plan the vineyards from scratch, they would lay them out almost as Van der Stel did centuries ago.

From Constantia a winding avenue lined with oak trees takes motorists up over Constantia Nek and down into Hout Bay. This pretty village, tucked away between the mountains in a secluded coastal area, is not served by the suburban railway line and, in its relative isolation, has developed a character all its own.

Once a year Hout Bay declares its independence, elects a president and issues passports to visitors. Cars sport bumper stickers proclaiming the 'Republic of Hout Bay'. It's all in a festive spirit, of course, but it does reflect the independent nature of the village and its people.

Hout Bay is home to a large community of writers, artists, potters and other craftspeople who find inspiration in the rural atmosphere away from the bustling city.

In the early days of the settlement of the Cape this area was a source of valuable timber for building houses and ships, hence the name, which means 'Wood Bay'.

When almost all the indigenous trees had been felled, the colonists began replacing them with the gracious oaks that are now a part of the area. They were originally intended to provide wood to make wine barrels for the fledgling wine industry in Constantia, but the wood turned out to be too porous for cask-making. In recent years residents have planted yellowwoods and other indigenous trees in the hope that their children will one day be able to see the kind of forest that gave the place its name.

Sheltered by the Sentinel peak on one side and Chapman's Peak on the other, Hout Bay provides a safe harbour for its fleet of fishing vessels. The village stretches up the valley from the beach towards Constantia Nek.

1

2

There was once a flurry of mining activity in the mountains above Hout Bay, and a chute was built to slide manganese ore down the mountainside and straight into the holds of cargo ships moored at a special ore jetty. There is a popular story that the first load of ore came hurtling down the chute with such force that it shot straight through the bottom of a waiting ship and sank her.

The mining, however, proved unprofitable and was abandoned. Relics of Hout Bay's mining days can be seen in the town's attractive little museum, and hikers in the surrounding hills still stumble across the remains of the old shafts and mining camps.

Also prominently featured in the Hout Bay museum is the story of the bay's fishing industry, for many years the area's biggest commercial occupation. Today the harbour boasts a modern processing factory which handles thousands of tons of fish and rock lobsters (known locally as 'crayfish' or 'kreef') each year for the country's gourmet restaurants. The harbour is also home to a fleet of trawlers, sailing boats and powerful, privately owned tunny craft.

1. Old Cape Dutch homesteads, like Kronendal in Hout Bay, remind visitors of a more gracious age.
2. Chapman's Peak drive, hewn from the rocky cliff face, is one of the most spectacular scenic drives in southern Africa.
3. The fishing industry has been modernised and mechanised, but there are still some who use traditional trek-boats, rowing through the surf to spread their long, hand-hauled nets.
4. When the snoek starts to run, anglers from all over the country congregate in Hout Bay.

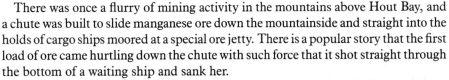

3

4

1. Groot Constantia was the birthplace of South Africa's wine tradition and visitors still stop here to taste wine and buy a bottle or two. This old cellar now houses an interesting wine museum.
2. Not all the grapes of Constantia go into the making of wine. Some fine table grapes are set out at the roadside to tempt the passer-by.
3. Autumn paints the Constantia vineyards in glowing copper and gold. Riding is a popular pastime in the valley.

SOUTHERN SUBURBS

HUDDLED BENEATH THE TOWERING EASTERN SLOPES of Table Mountain lie the 'southern suburbs' of Rosebank, Rondebosch, Newlands, Claremont, Constantia, Kenilworth, Wynberg and Plumstead. These are the old established residential areas where many of Cape Town's businessmen and their families have their homes. It's an area of serene, old, oak-lined avenues, large, sheltered gardens and elegant houses.

Much of this area was once the estate of the pioneer statesman, Cecil John Rhodes, who bequeathed it to the country he so loved. Rhodes' estate, known today as Groote Schuur Estate, occupies the mountain slopes above the southern suburbs, and provides passing motorists with unexpected glimpses of large antelope and wildebeest. The house, Groote Schuur, originally a storage barn built by Jan van Riebeeck, was re-modelled for Rhodes by the renowned architect Sir Herbert Baker. Above the university, a winding tarred road through pine forest takes you to the impressive Rhodes Memorial, which offers a breathtaking view across the Cape Flats to the distant Hottentot Holland Mountains. The Rhodes Memorial is a favourite evening spot for young lovers and has a cosy restaurant and tea-garden nearby.

The southern suburbs have a reputation for learning and research. Here you will find fine schools, the University of Cape Town, Groote Schuur teaching hospital, where the world's first heart transplant operation was performed, the South African Astronomical Observatory and Kirstenbosch Botanic Gardens.

Sport and recreation play an important role here, too. Newlands is the nationally acclaimed mecca of South African rugby enthusiasts, and the Newlands Cricket Ground is probably the most attractive in the country. Cynics like to say one of the reasons sports grounds were established in Newlands was the fact that one of the country's first breweries was established here. Sport and beer are seldom far apart. The brewery still flourishes, as the clear mountain water that flows in the Newlands Stream is considered ideal for brewing. The stream was also harnessed to drive a large mill, and the Josephine Mill has recently been restored after many years of disuse. Today the mill houses a fascinating museum, where you can buy excellent stone-ground flour, fresh from the water-driven millstones.

Two of South Africa's best known theatres, the Baxter Theatre and the Maynardville open-air theatre, offer a wide variety of entertainment. The Baxter's three stages are busy all year round, while the Maynardville Theatre offers an unforgettable annual Shakespeare production set on a tree-framed stage.

1. The University of Cape Town's campus is clustered neatly on the slopes of Devil's Peak.
2. Water lilies catch the sun in Claremont Gardens.
3. Students show their colours at the annual intervarsity rugby match at Newlands.
4. Karate breaks down barriers as two friends stroll home from classes.

1 2

3 4

The suburban railway line links these residential areas with the city and transports thousands of commuters, students and scholars to and from their places of work or learning each day. Tradition has it that the railway line marks the division between the social elite on the western side and those on the 'other side of the line' – the east. Properties to the east of the line are usually sold for rather less than their west-side counterparts.

A feature of this residential area is the large number of open public parks and gardens. The Newlands forest area is a favourite walking place for Capetonians, being within strolling distance or a short drive from many homes. Rhodes Memorial is also a popular walking place, and if you happen to be on foot here, you may very well see a fallow deer or two come up and sniff inquisitively at you in the hope of an edible handout.

Wynberg park is also an attractive recreational area, and Claremont Public Gardens are famed as a venue for wedding photographs. Every weekend you may see bridal groups here, posing against the lush greenery and flowers.

One of the Cape's biggest employers is the clothing industry, and there are few Cape Flats families that do not have at least one expert seamstress in their ranks. Weddings are times when sewing creativity is allowed free rein and many of the wedding gowns are spectacular. Brides, bridesmaids and pages pose for their pictures in a riot of satins and lace. These displays of finery are fast becoming a tourist attraction, and Claremont's wedding groups must now feature in the holiday snapshots of tourists all over the world.

1. Groote Schuur – Cecil John Rhodes's gift to the nation – was designed by the well-known architect Sir Herbert Baker.
2. The old Valkenburg manor house now houses a fashionable restaurant.
3. One of the Cape's best-known landmarks, Mostert's Mill, now stands in a well-groomed garden.
4. The symbol of physical energy, this spirited horseman at the Rhodes Memorial on Groote Schuur Estate looks out across the twinkling lights of the southern suburbs and Cape Flats.

1

2

1. The Baxter Theatre – breathtaking modern setting for a lively programme of year-round entertainment.
2. An old eland bull grazes peacefully in its paddock on Rhodes's Groote Schuur Estate while a busy egret hunts for insects.
3. Newly restored, the old Josephine Mill in Newlands is once again grinding out flour. The mill has been turned into a fascinating museum.
4. Kirstenbosch Botanic Gardens are known internationally for their collection of flora, and appreciated locally as a peaceful place for a weekend walk along flower lined forest paths.

3

4

On fine weekends Capetonians head for the outdoors, and the southern suburbs provide sunny entertainment for every taste.

1. Some enjoy a break from the busy city with a braai in the peaceful surroundings of the Newlands forest.
2. Others take to the air (with a little help from a horse) at Constantia.
3. Saturday afternoons in winter always find a good crowd rooting for 'Province' at Newlands Rugby Ground.
4. In summer the spectators move across the road and under the oaks for cricket.
5. And at Kenilworth, not far away, it's racing all year round. Everybody likes to bet a few rands on a horse for the 'Met', and any punter worth his salt knows exactly why his horse didn't win.

4 5

1. The wedding groups that gather in Claremont Public Gardens for their photographs present a weekly parade of fairytale fashions.
2. Wet roads and early dusk slow winter commuter traffic to a crawl.
3. A modern highway interchange draws lazy doodles on the landscape.
4. Produce markets are scattered throughout the Peninsula, and there's never a shortage of fresh fruit or vegetables.

CAPE POINT

AT THE SOUTHERNMOST TIP OF THE CAPE PENINSULA is one of the most powerful light-houses in the world. It perches on the rocky tip of the promontory and flashes out its 19-million candlepower warning signal to ships throughout the night.

The original lighthouse at Cape Point was situated high up, on the summit of the point, but the swirling fog often made it invisible to ships groping their way round the treacherous cape. The light was shrouded in mist on the fateful night in 1911 when the Portuguese liner *Lusitania* struck Bellows Rock and sank just off the point. Although only four people drowned, it was decided to move the lighthouse further down to its present site.

Hundreds of tourists visit Cape Point daily each summer and from the car park at the point walk up the steep stretch of concrete road to the site of the old lighthouse to stare down in fascination at the seething waters below. For those with more money than energy, there's a bus which must have one of the shortest regular routes of any bus in the world. It travels from the car park to the summit and back every few minutes – a distance of only a couple of hundred metres.

Oceans, of course, know no boundaries and the great masses of warm and cold water surge and flow where they must. Although geographers have decreed that the dividing line between the Atlantic and Indian Oceans is at Cape Agulhas, many people feel that the real meeting place of the two oceans is here at Cape Point. The warm waters of the Agulhas Current flow southward down the east coast of southern Africa, and it is at Cape Point that they meet the chilly Antarctic flow travelling northward. This collision not only makes the Agulhas Current lose its direction, but it deflects the cold water northward and westward to become the Benguela Current, which flows up the West Coast of Africa.

Standing at the tip of the Cape Peninsula, visitors can see the long line of white foam where the two currents clash. The force of the sea would have worn this point away much faster than it has were it not for Cape Point's foundation of granite. This granite is much harder than the Table Mountain sandstone which makes up the rest of the peninsula's spine. Even so, the fury of the sea has carved deep caves into the foot of the rocky cliffs.

1

3

1. Cape Point extends a crooked finger into the wild Atlantic.
2. Tumbled rocks and Cape fynbos are home to this family of red hartebeest in the Cape of Good Hope Nature Reserve.
3. A male ostrich surveys his seaside kingdom.

Cape Point has a wild and rugged beauty of its own, and much of this unspoiled character is due to the fact that the southern part of the peninsula has been declared a nature reserve. The 8 000 ha Cape of Good Hope Nature Reserve is inhabited by some of the species that once ranged freely over the whole of the Peninsula – ostriches, antelope, tortoises, zebra and baboons. Zoologists find the Cape Point baboon troop particularly interesting, as it is the only one known to have adapted its lifestyle to the seashore and its immediate environs. In addition to their normal diet of grubs, roots and insects, these baboons forage among the rocks at low tide and find plenty of seafood snacks to eat. Unfortunately, humans pose a serious threat to these unique animals by offering them food; this habit is turning some of these independent animals into beggars. Baboons which are accustomed to human handouts are known to attack people who do not offer them food. When this happens they have to be shot. It is sad that, in spite of all the warning notices placed about the reserve, humans continue to condemn the animals to death in this stupid way.

The reserve offers some very attractive drives, and there are several sheltered and accessible beaches where visitors can relax, picnic or swim. A copy of the cross, or *padrão*, planted by Bartholomeu Dias has been erected on a high point, but the site of the original *padrão* is not known. Recently, to mark the 500th anniversary of the event, a crew of Portuguese sailors re-enacted the famous voyage of Bartholomeu Dias in a replica of his little caravel, and erected another *padrão* – this time at a more likely site in Buffels Bay, a spot which would have given those early navigators a good landing place. Buffels Bay is a favourite picnic area for visitors to the reserve.

1. The most powerful lighthouse in the southern hemisphere flashes out its warning to ships at Cape Point.
2. A mother baboon finds the road a convenient place for a flea inspection and her baby takes it lying down. These Cape Point baboons have learned to forage among the rocks at low tide.
3. Only an occasional visitor to the Peninsula's shores, this young Southern elephant seal seems to resent having its nap disturbed by the photographer.

2

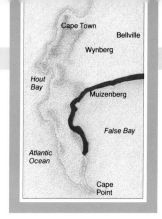

Cape Town
Bellville
Wynberg
Hout
Bay
Muizenberg
False Bay
Atlantic
Ocean
Cape
Point

FALSE BAY

'WIND, STRONG SOUTHERLY TO SOUTHEASTERLY, REACHING gale force over False Bay.' This is probably one of the most commonly used sentences in any South African radio or TV weather forecast, and one that is very appropriate too, for False Bay bears the full brunt of the southeasterly gales. In summer these winds come howling in through the mouth of the bay, between Cape Hangklip and Cape Point, often pushing mountainous seas ahead of them.

When Bartholomeu Dias rounded this wild cape five centuries ago and named it the Cape of Storms, he stayed only long enough to erect a stone cross, or *padrão*, somewhere near Cape Point before he scuttled off to rejoin his supply ship. Even today navigators regard Cape Point with great respect and give it a wide berth. Apart from the heaving seas, hidden reefs such as Bellows Rock and The Anvil lurk just below the surface, ready to smash any unwary boat to matchwood.

The rolling breakers that crash down on False Bay's Muizenberg beach, about 30 km north of Cape Point, make it a favourite spot for surfers. Further along, at nearby Kalk Bay, the towering waves that cascade over the harbour wall are an inspiration to photographers – and a nightmare for boat owners. In winter, however, when the prevailing wind is the northwesterly, False Bay provides some sheltered beaches and anchorages, and the wind flattens the sea, instead of churning it up. In the early days of sailing ships False Bay served as the winter anchorage of the sailing fleet, while Table Bay was considered safer in the summer months.

A large number of sharks cruise along the False Bay coastline, but there have been only one or two attacks recorded. This is probably because the waters teem with seals, which provide an abundant source of food for the sharks. The seals inhabit a small rocky island appropriately called Seal Island.

Cape fishermen traditionally hate the seals because they steal some of the catches, but any large-scale seal purges would undoubtedly upset the delicate balance of nature, and probably force the sharks to seek out bathers as a source of nourishment.

Each winter Southern Right whales cruise into the shelter of False Bay to mate and calve, and their appearance is greeted by long lines of parked cars and crowds of sightseers along the sea front. Simon's Bay and Fish Hoek were once the centres of a substantial whaling industry, but none of the local residents would consider harming these great and gentle creatures today.

1
3

1. Kalk Bay's attractive little harbour provides shelter to a small fleet of line boats.
2. When the south-easter blows, the harbour wall barely holds back the fury of the sea . . .
3. . . . but on calm days there's not even a ripple on the nearby St James pool.

1. At Muizenberg, the beach goes on and on, and in summer the water's seldom too cold for a swim.

2. Marina da Gama, near Muizenberg, offers waterside living to hundreds of families, and every home must have its boat.

3. This unusual aerial shot shows Muizenberg's modern pavilion in the foreground, while the bright blue of Zandvlei lagoon points the way to Table Mountain in the distance.

4. Surf lifesaving is a fiercely competitive sport as well as a valuable service. These determined young nippers go for the last flag during a competition on Fish Hoek beach.

The long sweep of False Bay is dotted with charming little coastal communities, one of which is the quaint naval village of Simon's Town, about half way between Cape Point and Muizenberg. Simon's Town has managed to preserve its historic character, but because it is also the main base of the South African Navy, much of it is closed to visitors for security reasons.

The sea front adjoining the yacht basin at Simon's Town has recently been improved to include a sheltered walkway with benches where visitors can relax and watch the comings and goings of hundreds of small pleasure craft. In nearby Jubilee Square is the statue of a dog called Just Nuisance, which became famous as the constant friend of British naval ratings during the Second World War. The life story of Just Nuisance is portrayed in a special section of the Simon's Town Museum.

Further along the coastline is Fish Hoek – a little 'dry' hamlet best known for the fact that no alcoholic beverages may be sold within its municipal boundaries. Tradition has it that this regulation originated when ox-wagons used to carry supplies from Cape Town to the fleet wintering in Simon's Town, and had to spend a night in Fish Hoek on the way. The hospitality was generous and the drivers often became so drunk during their stopover that they couldn't control their ox teams the next day: many wagons overturned on the tricky winding road, spilling the precious provisions into the sea, much to the irritation of the hungry sailors. When freehold land was eventually granted in Fish Hoek it was done so on the strict condition that no liquor was to be sold in the area. Thirsty residents have tried to change the regulations several times, but their efforts have been met with strong opposition from defenders of the town's traditions, and the matter has always been dropped.

4

1. A hardy angler braves the chill morning mist to cast his line into the surf at Strandfontein near Muizenberg, while a group of gulls waits expectantly.

2. For those who go to sea in the line boats from Kalk Bay, catches are sometimes good, often disappointing. When the snoek are biting, times are good for everybody, but even a small one like this will help to feed the family. Anglers say the catches are improving since trawlers were banned from False Bay.

3. On a calm summer evening the lights of Kalk Bay, Fish Hoek and Simon's Town form a sparkling necklace round the water's edge.

3

In sharp contrast, Kalk Bay, just next door, is home to a fleet of line-fishing boats and weekends are rollicking times when the drink flows freely and the language turns as blue as the sea. Sometimes fists fly and knives flash, and Monday's crews are decorated with swollen eyes and bandaged heads. When the snoek are biting throngs of buyers flock to the harbour as the boatmen auction their catch, still accepting bids in 'bobs' – a reminder of the days when a shilling was a useful sum of money. A unique feature of Kalk Bay is its railway station, which has an excellent seafood restaurant right on the platform, overlooking the sea.

Muizenberg, once the holiday resort of the very rich, still has its row of large and ornate, but sadly faded, mansions along the beach front. Most of these splendid Edwardian vacation homes have now been divided into holiday flats for the rather less opulent. Muizenberg still remains a popular place for holidaymakers for, like most False Bay resorts, the beaches are excellent for swimming and surfing and the sea is pleasantly warm – unlike the icy waters on the Peninsula's west coast, usually referred to as the 'Atlantic side'. In fact, both sides of the Cape Peninsula are lapped by the Atlantic, as the official dividing line between the Atlantic and Indian Ocean is at Cape Agulhas, far to the east.

From Muizenberg the smooth sandy beaches of the False Bay coastline arc gently eastward for several kilometres and then change into a line of craggy white cliffs that reach up vertically from the sea, providing a home for thousands of sea birds.

At the eastern end of this stretch of shoreline is The Strand, the traditional holiday resort for Boland farmers. The Strand has grown from a few thatched 'strandhuisies' to a high-rise flatland dotted with fine hotels and restaurants. The beach provides particularly safe swimming, as the sand slopes gently and the waves are rarely rough.

Gordon's Bay, not too far away, has one of the most attractive small harbours in the Cape, and is home to a large fleet of privately owned ski-boats and a growing number of yachts. Here the beaches end and the coastline becomes rocky and steep, extending southward to Cape Hangklip, the towering sentinel which guards the southern approach to False Bay.

1

On False Bay's shores, long stretches of white sand provide plenty of space for sports of all kinds.

1. A surfer adds a flying flash of colour to the face of a breaker on Kalk Bay reef.
2. An early morning gallop on the sand helps to build stamina and muscle. Sleek thoroughbred horses are a common sight on this stretch of beach.
3. Low tide and a bright evening moon create the perfect practice green for this seaside golfer on Fish Hoek beach.

Overleaf: Gordon's Bay Harbour has become a popular boating centre with a growing fleet of cruising and racing yachts, as well as powerful fishing craft. In the golden sunset a lone canoeist reviews the fleet.

2

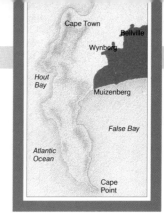

CAPE FLATS

MENTION THE CAPE FLATS TO THE AVERAGE CAPETONIAN and you will probably conjure up a picture of crowded squalor, squatter shacks and wind-blown sand. The area is often in the news as the unofficial home of thousands of black families who have moved from rural areas in search of work.

But there are other faces to this broad expanse of low-lying ground. Much of it is valuable agricultural land, where industrious farmers, many of German extraction, produce a considerable quantity of fresh vegetables, milk and poultry for the people of Cape Town.

There are recreational areas like Zeekoevlei, with its well established yacht club and public boating facilities, and Rondevlei, a bird sanctuary that provides a haven of tranquillity untouched by the rush of the city which surrounds it.

The Cape Flats, more than any other area of the Cape Peninsula, has seen great changes. When the first sailing ships called at the Cape, one of their urgent needs was firewood for the galley stoves. As soon as ships had anchored in Table Bay, shore parties were sent to collect as much firewood as they could. In those early days the Cape Flats were dotted with gnarled and stunted shrubs that had grown tough in the harsh and windy environment. Their stumps provided excellent fuel for the ships' cooking and were uprooted eagerly without consideration for the effect this would have on the environment. The eventual result was that the flats were stripped of their trees. Before long the flats became a desolate place of shifting dunes where not even a road could last long without being covered by the fine, wind-driven sand.

Eventually the authorities found a way to halt the shifting sands of the Cape Flats – they imported the Port Jackson wattle, a hardy Australian tree that thrived on the flats. The Port Jackson did so well, in fact, that it started turning into a problem far worse than the shifting sands had been. It encroached on vast areas of indigenous fynbos, threatening and destroying it in many places. Today, this encroachment, and that by other alien vegetation, is a major ecological problem. The Cape's fynbos is recognised internationally as one of the great floral kingdoms of the world, and its destruction by the wattles has prompted ecologically-minded Capetonians to declare war on the species.

Many conservationists join weekend 'hacks', armed with chain saws, axes and hatchets to chop back the invaders. Recently an Australian insect was introduced to the wattle areas in the hope that it would slow the spread of these fast-growing plants. In its native land the insect attacks wattles by forming galls which eventually kill the trees, but it will be many years before we know whether this experiment succeeds.

1. At Philippi, precise rows of well-tended vegetables grow for Cape tables.
2. Graffiti provides a bright backdrop for an informal Cape Flats concert.
3. Harvest time provides work for many as the bags are filled for market.

1

On the Cape Flats modern suburban living rubs shoulders with 'Third World' Africa.

1. In every community, children play their own traditional games. These Mitchell's Plain children apparently have rules far too complicated for an outsider to understand.
2. Mitchell's Plain – neat suburbia created on the Cape Flats dunes.
3. In many Cape Flats areas trade is an informal business – and businesses can't get much more informal than this!
4. Often in the news, Crossroads squatter township is a headache for the authorities, but a home to thousands of families.

2

Another major change to the face of the Flats has been the establishment of Mitchell's Plain, a huge, modern residential area, one of several designed to cope with Cape Town's serious housing shortage. Where, only a few years ago, there was nothing but a tangle of Port Jackson thickets, there are now busy streets, shopping centres, schools, cinemas, churches, mosques and thousands of new homes.

While this urban development has been rapid, the town planners insist it is nowhere near rapid enough: the Flats communities are among the fastest-expanding in the country, and even with the impressive building rate, it looks as though the housing gap is widening alarmingly.

Some planners say the real crisis facing South Africa is not a political one. It is simply the fact that the urban population is increasing faster than society can provide services and jobs. Nowhere is this more graphically illustrated than on the Cape Flats.

But in spite of its problems, the Cape Flats manages to maintain a merry face. The people here provide their own entertainment. Any open area is fine for an informal soccer match, or even a few rounds of boxing. Religious revival meetings attract large crowds, and business is conducted on every street corner. Hawkers sell vegetables and fresh snoek from False Bay, and haggling is loud and raucous. Anybody who has a horse and cart is in the transport business, and almost anybody with a minibus is a taxi driver.

Brushes with the law are everyday events, often providing excellent entertainment for onlookers. But there is a serious side to this too. Crimes of violence are distressingly common on the Flats, as they are in any overcrowded area. This is a major problem for urban planners and no workable solution has yet been found.

1

2

1. Large families mean large loads of laundry. In some areas the bright washday banners add colour to an otherwise drab scene. For some, a back fence makes a convenient washing line . . .

2. . . . but where there are no fences, a length of wire links two shacks and a comfortable chair lets the children enjoy the sunshine while keeping a watchful eye on the drying clothes.

3. Soccer is a favourite pastime. Almost every patch of vacant ground sports a pair of sagging goalposts, and there's never a shortage of players to make up a team.

4. In crisis times community workers help to provide food, shelter and medical care. The Cape Flats have seen more than their share of crises.

1

1. A little initiative, a horse and a home built cart and you're in business. There are enough customers who need a cartage job, or who have some junk to throw out.

2. There's always plenty of entertainment on the flats. An impromptu boxing match gathers an enthusiastic group of Saturday spectators.

3. Like shopping centres everywhere, this one on Mitchell's Plain hums with activity on a Saturday morning.

2

1. A curtain of stormy sunshine creates a backdrop for a board-sailer at Zeekoevlei.
2. Others take to the air for their entertainment.
3. 'Gosh! How does he do it?' Solemn pelicans gather at the water's edge to watch the human antics.
4. Across the flats at DF Malan Airport, an incoming airliner approaches the evening runway.

4

NORTHERN SUBURBS

TO THE NORTHEAST OF CAPE TOWN LIES A SPRAWLING area of smart modern homes, tall office blocks and factories. These 'northern suburbs' of Bellville, Durbanville and Parow have grown rapidly in recent years. In fact, Bellville is no suburb at all – it was officially given city status more than a decade ago.

Towns are established for a strange variety of reasons, but the beginnings of modern-day Bellville were humble indeed. In the early days of the settlement of the Cape, it took a full two days to travel by ox-wagon from Cape Town to the agricultural hamlet of Stellenbosch; two very tough days of travel along a rutted and crude road which crossed the wind-driven sands of the Cape Flats. Any wagon which strayed from the road was likely to find itself firmly stuck in the soft sand. One of the few places where the ground alongside the road was hard enough to allow a wagon to turn out was a place about 12 miles (19 km) from Cape Town. It was known by the wagon drivers as 'Hardekraaltjie'. There was a small stream nearby and the spot became the regular overnight stopping place for the wagons. Governor Simon van der Stel spent several nights camped there on his frequent trips to Stellenbosch.

When an embryo village started growing near this outspan spot, it had no official name and was called, simply, 'Twaalf Myl' (Twelve miles). By the mid-19th century, railway planners surveying a new line to Eerste River decided to call the little village D'Urban Road. The name was never officially used, although the railways did erect a signboard saying 'D'Urban Road', which stood for years after the village was officially called Bellville.

The name Bellville was given to the village in 1861 by a Government proclamation, in honour of the Scottish-born chief surveyor of the Cape, Charles Davidson Bell. Bell was also a renowned artist, and designed the famous Cape of Good Hope triangular stamps, which are now highly prized by philatelists.

Today the old 12th milestone can still be seen at the intersection of Voortrekker and Durban Roads in Bellville, and Hardekraaltjie lives on, appropriately, as the name of the popular Bellville caravan park, where modern travellers can outspan in much more comfort than Van der Stel ever enjoyed.

1. Bellville children enjoy the sunshine, surrounded by the fast-growing city.
2. Religious life plays an important role in the northern suburbs.
3. Tygerberg shoppers browse in an airy, modern shopping complex.
4. Drum majorettes are popular and inter-school competition is very keen.

The northern suburbs have become one of the fastest-developing areas of the Cape Peninsula. Here you will find Tygerberg Hospital, the largest in the region. Tygerberg is a teaching hospital linked to the University of Stellenbosch. The area also has one of the largest and most modern shopping centres in the Cape, a giant complex of railway workshops, a business centre every bit as busy as that of Cape Town and several excellent Afrikaans and English-medium schools. The Tygerberg has a range of good restaurants almost as varied as that of Sea Point.

In Bellville's industrial area, factories produce everything from agricultural machinery and irrigation equipment to paint and ocean-going yachts. And tucked away among the Tygerberg hills are several old-established wine estates, where some of the country's finest wines are produced.

This is a vibrant, fast-moving area that is often considered by residents of Cape Town's elite southern areas to be brash and upstart. Indeed, as recently as the 1950s the area was little more than a rural village. The leap from hamlet to prosperous city has been amazingly quick, but the young city does have its roots deeply planted in the history of the Cape. And while the rest of the Peninsula sometimes appears to be nodding off to sleep, the Tygerberg is very wide awake. Today it is hard to believe that Bellville began as just a little patch of hard earth in a wilderness of shifting sand.

1. Durbanville is an interesting mix of urban and rural life. In the foreground is the racecourse.
2. This bright, modern students' centre serves the University of the Western Cape.
3. Bellville's modern city centre.
4. A midday lull at the Bellville bus terminus – it's busy at rush hour, though.
5. Bellville's War Memorial.
6. Busy Voortrekker Street, which links Bellville with the Mother City, also passes through Parow.

A DAY AWAY

SURROUNDED AS THEY ARE BY SO MUCH NATURAL BEAUTY, Cape Town's people have developed a great love of the countryside. Summer weekends see streams of vehicles heading out of the city, bound for the mountains, the flowers or nearby coastal resorts. Everybody has a favourite getaway place, and one of the enchantments of the Cape is that it seldom takes more than a couple of hours to get there.

In Britain spring is traditionally heralded by the first cuckoo, but in the Cape it's the flowers of the West Coast that signal the end of the long, wet winter. In some places these wild flowers form an unbroken carpet of glowing colour as far as the eye can see. Some towns, such as Clanwilliam, hold an annual wild flower show, and hundreds of tour buses take groups of visitors to the multicoloured fields of flowers. Tour companies have flower spotters in each West Coast village, so they can plan their routes to offer the most spectacular displays.

But if it is the flowers that lure people to the West Coast, it's the Southern Right whales that call them to Walker Bay. In late winter and early spring these great, gentle mammals appear close to the shore at Hermanus, and visitors line the clifftops for a glimpse of them as they surface to blow their plumes of mist into the air. Hermanus is a fascinating seaside town where many of Cape Town's fashionable set have holiday homes. The beaches here are not particularly good, but city people pay high prices to own a piece of land between the craggy, brooding mountains and the rocky coastline.

The area around Hermanus is famous for its wide variety of indigenous flora, and particularly for its proteas. In the fynbos reserve attractive mountainside walks not only offer breathtaking views over the bay, but also the chance to see the spectacular natural display of flowers and wild shrubs. Walker Bay has always been a favourite fishing place, but like so much of the South African coastline, old anglers say it has been overexploited and is nothing like it was in the 'good old days'. A walk through the town's old fishing harbour museum is a must for all first-time visitors to Hermanus. Ah yes, they really did land some big 'uns in those days.

Stellenbosch and Paarl, two of the Cape's best known wine producing areas, are less than an hour's drive from the city centre. Most of Cape Town's wine lovers have their favourite cellars on the Wine Route, and travel out from time to time to taste the latest vintage and stock up with reasonably priced wines. In spite of ever increasing costs, the Cape's wines are still cheap and there's a special charm about buying a case from the farm.

At Franschhoek, vineyards and mountains provide a tranquil rural atmosphere only a short drive from the centre of Cape Town.

1

2

3

Stellenbosch wine farmers were the first in the country to establish a formal wine route to attract tourists and promote the wines of their area. Today the Stellenbosch Wine Route offers far more than just wine. Several farms have established restaurants where visitors can enjoy a glass of wine and a meal under the old oak trees or in a warm country atmosphere. Some farmers have opened farm shops, where they sell a wide range of produce, cheese and wine-related mementoes.

Several cellars offer conducted tours, which give the uninitiated an insight into the fine craft of wine-making, and at least one farm has established a small wine museum. Daily coach tours in summer bring thousands of visitors to the Wine Route to taste the wines and enjoy the old-world rural atmosphere.

Hiking remains one of the Cape's favourite outdoor activities, and the craggy Boland mountains attract many weekend hikers from the city. Fortunately there's still plenty of space for everybody, and the extensive hiking trail network enables you to get away from it all and experience the awesome splendour and solitude of the un-spoiled mountains. For those who like their leisure wet and wild, the Breede and Berg Rivers offer exciting canoeing possibilities, where tranquil stretches of peaceful water alternate with roaring rapids that are fast and wild enough to test the reflexes of even the most experienced paddler.

But if it's just peace and rest you want, there are plenty of sleepy country and coastal villages where nothing happens all year round. And nothing is plenty for some. Mountains, rivers and beaches, walks and wine – surely few cities in the world can offer such a diversity just a short drive from the bustle of the business centre.

303

1. The patchwork of the Paarl Valley stretches up to the mountains.
2. Ponds of 'waterblommetjies' provide gourmets with a favourite Cape delicacy.
3. A curved ribbon of road leads to the new Huguenot Tunnel.
4. The whitewashed Dutch Reformed church points its steeple at the cloudless Paarl sky.
5. Paarl is the starting point of the annual Berg River Canoe marathon.

Overleaf: Waterblommetjies' watery harvest.

5

1. The farms around Stellenbosch are famed for their fine grapes and wine, but also produce other, less glamorous, crops like these cabbages.
2. A cow grazes quietly in a pasture as a tractor sets off for the day's work.
3. A team of efficient scarecrows keep watch over a field of strawberries near Stellenbosch. Some modern scarecrows even arrive at work by scooter! The annual crop of scarecrows has become a regular attraction for delighted visitors to the farm.

2

3

1. Autumn is a spectacular season in the Cape, when vineyards are touched with mellow magic.
2. Harvest time is the busiest season of the wine farmers' year – and often the most anxious. Grapes must be harvested at exactly the right ripeness, and a change of weather can spell the difference between a great vintage and an ordinary one.
3. Agricultural land is valuable and on many farms only the smallest area is reserved for living space.

1. In Stellenbosch's historic Dorp Street almost every building bears the distinctive bronze plaque of the Historical Monuments Commission.

2. Bicycles are a popular form of transport in this university town and several bicycle dealers do a brisk trade, keeping some old student cycles on the road year after year.

3. In Oom Samie's famous trading store you can step back into the past and discover a world of rolled tobacco, home remedies and home-made jams, pickles and handcrafts. Prices, however, have moved with the times.

1. Bontebok in the Postberg Nature Reserve stare curiously at the camera.
2. A sea of wheat stretches all the way to the Overberg mountains.
3. When snow falls on the mountains of the Boland, Capetonians can feel it in their bones.
4. An old tradition with a slight difference – the quarry is not a live fox.
5. It may take a little effort to get to the snow, but a snowman makes it worth while.

Overleaf: At Hermanus, sunset turns the rocks to gold.

3

4

5

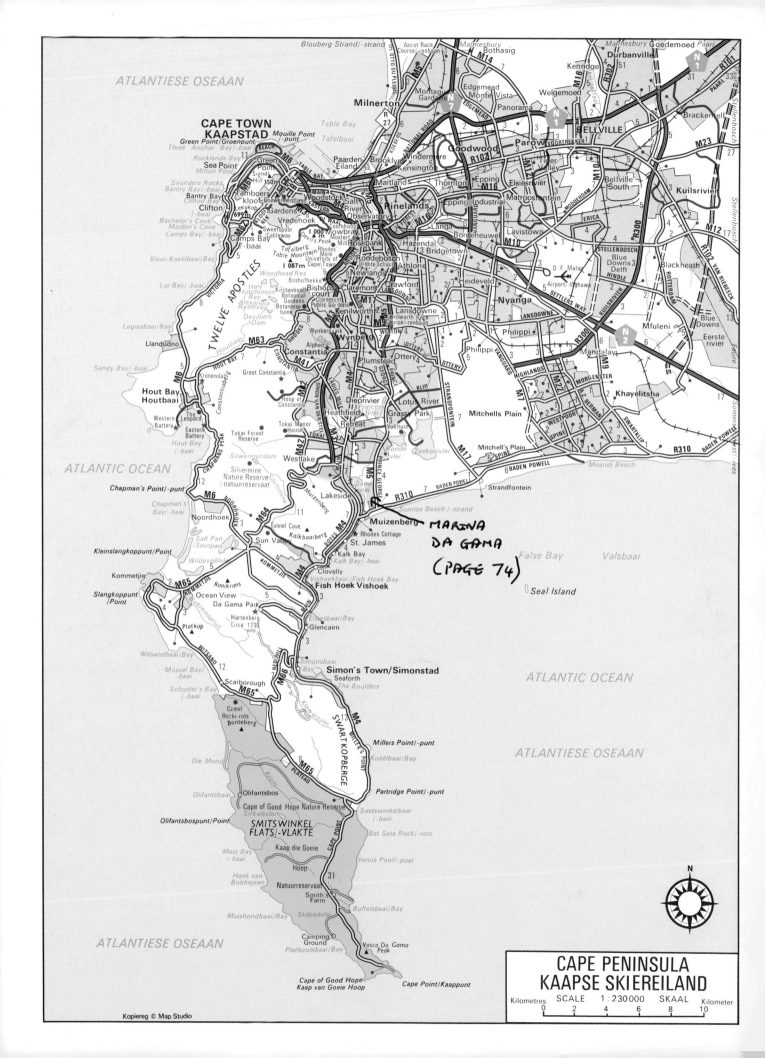

CAPE PENINSULA
KAAPSE SKIEREILAND